debbie tucker green

Theatre includes: *stoning mary* (Royal Court); *generations* (Young Vic); *trade* (RSC); *born bad* (Hampstead); *dirty butterfly* (Soho).

Television includes: *spoil*.

Radio includes: *handprint*, *freefall*, *to swallow*.

Awards include: Olivier Award for Most Promising Newcomer 2004, for *born bad*.

debbie tucker green

random

NICK HERN BOOKS

London

www.nickhernbooks.co.uk

A Nick Hern Book

random first published in Great Britain in 2008 as a paperback original by Nick Hern Books Limited, 14 Larden Road, London W3 7ST, in association with the Royal Court Theatre, London

Reprinted 2009

random copyright © 2008 debbie tucker green

debbie tucker green has asserted her right to be identified as the author of this work

Cover illustrations by Russ Mills
Cover designed by Ned Hoste, 2H

Typeset by Nick Hern Books, London
Printed in the UK by CPI Antony Rowe, Chippenham, Wiltshire

A CIP catalogue record for this book is available from the British Library

ISBN 978 1 85459 556 0

random was first performed at the Royal Court Jerwood Theatre Downstairs, London, on 7 March 2008, performed by Nadine Marshall, and directed by Sacha Wares.

Characters

SISTER
BROTHER
MUM
DAD
TEACHER
and others

One Black actress plays all characters.

Dialogue in ( ) is to be spoken.

Dialogue in [ ] is intention, not to be spoken.

Italicised sentences in ( ) are stage directions.

Part Two is listed in the text; however, the play is to be performed straight through without any break.

This text went to press before the end of rehearsals and so may differ slightly from the play as performed.

PART ONE

SISTER
... And the su'un in the air –
in the room –
in the day –
like the
shadow of a shadow feelin...
off-key – I...
look the clock. Eyeball it.
It looks me back.
Stare the shit down –
it stares me right back.

(*Beat.*)

... Till it blinked first – loser.
Then changes its time... 7.37.
a.m.

So I –
give it my back –
roll on my front –
flex under the duvet
and lie there on the reluctant to get up –
a rubbish night's sleep
a restless night's sleep
for no reason at all.
Birds bitchin their birdsong outside.
People already on road.
Dogs in their yards barkin the shit outta
the neighbourhood.

This ent a morning to be peaceful
and the somethin in the air –
in the room –
in this day –

mekin mi shiver –
even tho my single duvet
is holdin onto me like my man –
who still don't phone –
should be.

Sun strugglin to be seen outside –
playin hide and seek with the clouds
like iss joke –
like iss shy –
losin its own game –
like we don't matter.
One a them, put that on – not that – not
that – that on – days a clothin confusion.
Truss mi.

BROTHER   7.38.
a.m.
Lay bad. Slept bad. Stretch (*choops*) –
don't help.
Birds sweetin their birdsong outside. Nice.
People already on road.

Neighbourhood Stafs barkin the shit outta
the area.
Sun doin what I do –
five more minutes –
ent ready for the up.
And the su'un in the air –
in the day –
in my room…

7.41.
a.m.

Iss now –
after the night –
iss now –
after all night –
iss only now – after night done and

daylight reach
that sleep comes to find me.
My turn.

SISTER No worries bout rushin the bathroom –
Mum done long time –
Dad not doin day shifts –
and that '*thing*' ent never up before me –
step to his room – knock –
don't lissen to hear nu'un –
don't wanna hear nu'un –
don't care –
go in anyway.

'... You awake?'

(*Beat.*)

'You awake – '

BROTHER this one can't be inna my dream.

SISTER 'You awake – '

BROTHER nightmare.

(BROTHER *kisses his teeth.*)

SISTER 'I can borrow y'phone?'

BROTHER 'I'm sleepin.'

SISTER 'This room stinks – '

BROTHER 'come outta it then – '

SISTER 'so I can borrow y'phone – an' you ent
sleepin – you sleepin? – how come yu
sleepin all now? – mek mi borrow your
phone – '

BROTHER 'you credit-less – your problem.'

SISTER 'Wanna use your sim in it – ennit – '

BROTHER	'find a next phone – or a next man yeh?'
	(*Beat.*)
SISTER	'… I'ma 'llow that. Yeh?'
	(BROTHER *kisses his teeth.*)
	'Thass an answer? Thass your answer?'
	(BROTHER *kisses his teeth.*)
BROTHER	'An' close back mi door.'
SISTER	Why he
	think I wanna –
	why he think I wanna be in his room that
	[*s*]*tink*.
	Why he think I wanna be –
	in his room –
	with him – that stinkin bwoy longer than
	mi haf to – ask me.
	8.13. Step downstairs.
	Kitchen radio don't tune [in] right.
	Little breakfast Mum mek, catch.
	Juice finish.
	Tea too hot.
	Mum makin like it don't matter.
MUM	Porridge with black bits –
	bu'n up bits in –
	don't taste nice.
	Iss her cookin that normally catch –
	but…
	something ketch me out today.
	I see her watchin –
	I stir it in
	style it out
	watch ar back –
	till she turn and face she own bowl a
	breakfas someting –

with ar smile –
and I eat my bowl a cornmeal
with its black bits in anyhow.

She don't want none.
She late down –
don't think I notice
that she nah mek the time fe a proper
'eat enough' –
a proper – 'drink enough' –
of a morning.
She still tink bein young –
is bein invincible.
She still tink seh she young…
(*amused*) She like me.
She'll learn.
Like me.

An' she dress like iss summer
while spring still strugglin.
She see me lookin
and find su'un interestin
to face in ar bowl a cornflake.
She'll learn.

8.25.
'That whatchu wearin?'

SISTER	'Yeh.'
MUM	She wan' go up an' change.
	'You sure?'
SISTER	'Yeh.'
MUM	She not.
	'Y'warm enough?'
SISTER	'… Yeh.'
MUM	She won't be.
	'Y'sure?'

SISTER	'Mum.'
MUM	'Y'man ring yu?'
SISTER	*'Mum!'*
MUM	Thass all I said –
SISTER	So I… left – I leave – get my shit together an' gone. Not eaten enough – not drunk enough – (she don't need to know that) not time. I… step. To work. Open up and meet the day – and… ent nearly got enough clothes on neither. Iss cold. Truss mi. 8.32.
MUM	(*amused*) Now she garn. So I… dash mi dish a burn. But I – save enough in the pot f'him. Fe Junior. For when him come down. If him come down. … Him should be down… (MUM *listens.*) (MUM *shivers.*)
SISTER	You spose to rule y'dog. Y'dog ent spose to rule yu. I see them Staf-Bull sportin youts

bein dragged by their beas's –
tryin an' stylin to look like they not.

8.45.
Everybody on the catch out
in the confusion a what to wear –
nobody gonna [ad]mit to bein wrong –
lookin wrong –
sweatin off –
or shiverin.

Them thass too hot
tryinta mask it lookin cool.
Them thass proper cold
stylin out they shivers –
big pops –
young she's –
young bucks
an' shorties.
Everybody ketch out
with this…
(*gestures weather*)

(*Beat.*)

9 o'clock.
I reach.
I…
nod my hellos –
smile…
cos I'm paid to.
Sit next to them
that I have to –
sippin my nasty cold cuppa work su'un –
to be sociable –
while I…
dream on the monthly cheque –
only thing thass keeping me here –
cos the Sallys –
the Johns –

the Deepaks –
the Janes –
the smalls talk –
the who did that –
the who saw that bein done –
the who did what last night.
The who woulda done it better
if that was them –
and the who they was diding it with –
truss mi…
None a that's keeping me here…

9.03.
Only.
I…
clock my off phone –
(if I can't phone my man on the 'find out'.
My man ent able to phone me on the
'excuse')
set my face
and start my work.

BROTHER	'Anythin to eat – '
MUM	Like iss hotel.
BROTHER	'Anythin to eat?'
MUM	Like mi favour landlady.
BROTHER	'What is there to – '
MUM	'Porridge.'
BROTHER	'That?'
MUM	'That.'
BROTHER	'That ent – '
MUM	'It is.'
BROTHER	'… Got black bits in.'

MUM

'Yu late down, porridge ha fe bu'n.'
Heh.
Him watch the pot
watches me watchin
sights the juice – carton done
draws some milk –
only glasses it
cah him see me watchin.
Leaves out the empty glass
leaves out the still some in it milk
gives it the kiss on the side a *my* head
like I used to give it the kiss
on the side a *his*
when him was about ten…
Even then him would wipe it off –
with a smile –
thatchu couldn't.

I wipe his off
so him smile. He laugh – nearly –
as close as mi a go get from the big ting
that he is –
from the teenager he is –
but I'll tek it.

BROTHER

'She gone?'

MUM

'She gone.'

Him tek up him tings an' offs to school –
with a –

BROTHER

'Laters Mum.'

MUM

Like that'll do.
Him noh care that him n'eat enough –
nah do a proper 'drink enough' –
still tink bein young –
is bein… [invincible].
Ask mi –
how yu can mek a uniform look…

not like a uniform…
a tie look –
not like it spose to tie –
a trouser fit –
how you wannit to –
not how it meant to – *so low*?
A shirt flex, informal –
when it doin iss best to formalise?
A shoe look more like a sneak –
than a sneak look like a trainer?
A uniform look –
not how it intended –
but how yu intend?
… How them do that?

(MUM *smiles*.)

Heh.

BROTHER

She on a su'un of a mornin
if she down to bunnin porridge
yu haf'ee *try* to do that man –
that shit don't juss happen.
She think I ent eatin enough –
ent drinkin enough –
she gotta do betta than that black-up
pot of nastiness.

9.10.
Pass the Staf-Bull bredrins –

'Wha'gwa'an.'

Pass the youts doin the same as me –

'Move.'

They as late as me.

'Ennit tho.'

Pass thru the newsagent that doin pre-
school breakfast business.

'Alright.'

Walkers Ready Salted fill the gap.
Coke's finest juicin the cracks.
Girls bein loud –
bredrins bein louder –

'Yeh – yu nice – you – not y'frien' – *you*'

sight my mans them –

'Bless.'

An' step to the schoolhouse
phonin the sour-face sis –
that I got
who still screwin bout my mobile –
that I got
holdin a grudge –
how she do
feel to show her a little love –
how iss done
but her phone's lock off…
So leave her a stink message instead.

MUM   I…
flick on the Fern and the Phil –
pon the kitchen TV set
look to the places and spaces
where my big two babies were
and set to clearing and cleanin what's left
behind.
Like I'm their keeper –
their cleaner –
their… heh
their mum.

And as her cornflake bowl
is scrape free of wet leftovers
and the dregs of the drinks
is sunk inna the sink

and the crumbs and the marks and milk
and signs of their mess
is wiped away...
The sun breaks out
and decides it's gonna show.
'My days.'

Fern and Phil still a chat them shit
still deep inna it –
the clean up kitchen
waits for the next time –
the washin-up drips to it's dry –
the sun shoots a shine thru the window –
I watch it –
I...
see it.
But –
nah feel it.
Cah... still I ketch a –
shiver of the shadow of the shadow of the
day.

SISTER   How these people come to work?
                      How these people come to work –
                      but don't wanna work?
                      Ask me?!
                      If you don't wanna work –
                      don't come –
                      nah –
                      if you come –
                      don't reach cos your only reason is
                      to come by *me* and chat *your* shit
                      inna *my* ears
                      bout how much you hate it.
                      I hate it.
                      Hate them.
                      Hate hearin –
                      Sally's

John's
Deepak's
and Jane's
business.
Hate havin to hear it – day in day out –
why they think I wanna hear that?
Why they think I care – and if Sally flicks
that hair of *hers*
near *my* face –
again...
truss –
mi.
[They] chat their shit to me –
[they] sit back
they chattin their shit to me
spectin me to –
chat shit back to them –
spectin me to –
chat *my* shit back to them
I got friends f'that –
I got –
fambily f'that –
truss mi –
I got me a *man* fe that...
Well.
Sort of.

BROTHER   Little bit late better'n not at all.
            Little bit late better than not [at all] – yeh?
            Soon come betta than don't come – y'get –
            sometime betta than never –
            can't tell me it ent –
            rock up an' reach a little ten minutes down
            – yeh?

TEACHER   'Twenty'

BROTHER   she says. But I'm there.

TEACHER   'Not good enough – '

BROTHER   she says – but I reach.

TEACHER   'Just.'

BROTHER   She says.
               Givin me grief
               when there's others –
               truss [mi]
               others –
               on the in behind me – y'get? –
               diggin their Walkers breakfast
               out their teet still.
               Now.
               I aint that – I ent that bad
               blastin me out –
               an' tellin me iss for my own good –
               when there's others worss!
               Blatant.

               (*dry*) 'Know yu miss me Miss'

TEACHER   'Siddown'

BROTHER   's'only juss a ten – '

TEACHER   'twenty – '

BROTHER   'I can't help it if you missin me after – '

TEACHER   'Sit. Down.'

BROTHER   ' – after a ten minutes – '

TEACHER   '*twenty*.'

               (*Beat*.)

BROTHER   See.
               I give ar joke
               even when she try all her –
               hardness and teacherness –
               an' teacher-trainin tactics –
               we still gotta little –

TEACHER   'SIT. DOWN!'

BROTHER   She say I got potential –
            I *know* I got potential –
            but come on now
            bare blastin me out in fronta my...
            when I was only ten –

TEACHER   '*twenty*'

BROTHER   late. Come on now...
            Don't mek mi have to say somethin.

SISTER   Sally... told John
            some su'un bout Deepak...
            that Deepak never want John to know
            and never know Sally
            was tellin him.
            Jane see it all –
            and ent sayin shit –
            Deepak vex –
            John actin ignorant –
            Sally sayin she sorry –
            twistin her hair ends with the stress ar
            mout' put her in – bout askin me:
            What do I think?

            (SISTER *kisses her teeth.*)

MUM   'Wha' yu want fe dinner?'

            (*Beat.*)

            'Is whatchu want fe yu dinner?'

            (*Beat.*)

            Him still asleep –
            so him a go get what him given.
            Heh.
            So mi look to put mi su'un on

to meet an' greet the outside worl' in –
but iss…
One a them – put that – not that – *that* on
weather days a clothin confusion
cah the sun still nah lookin like iss sure.
Hmm.
So mi dress –
mi check –
mi re-dress again an' –

DAD   Lamb.

MUM   Hmm?

DAD   Lamb.

MUM   Hmph.
           The dead awake.

SISTER   Dad the kinda dad who…
           don't say much.
           Unless he have to.
           Who…
           don't say nuthin –
           unless he want to –
           who –
           won't say anythin
           unless he feel to –
           a –
           'Wha' yu want?
           Wha' yu seh?
           Wha' yu do?
           Where yu deyah?'
           Usually goddit covered, y'get.

           He the kinda dad who a –
           'hmm'
           can make you smile.
           A silence…
           can make you look

a pause
can make you confess
truss mi –
a eyebrow
can make you nervous.
He the kinda dad who kinda…
he kinda…
kind.

Deepak lunchin on his own –
wanna know if I wanna join him.
Sally still lookin sorrowful –
sippin on her SlimFast *fast*
her hair juss lookin –
a mess a stress now –
Jane chattin shit –
nervous bout who to ally herself wid –
tho nobody don't really want her –
and John chicken out
and gone for the take out –
Me?
I lie.
Say I wanna work thru lunch…
On my ownsome.

Morning done.
At last.

1 o'clock.

MUM	Why yu can't walk inna ones and twos?
	That gone outta fashion?
	Pon street – why yu can't walk inna –
	yu noh haf fe bunch up
	crowd up
	loaft street
	inna – posse
	crew
	pack

or whatever dem wan' call it.
Why dem cyan' walk inna ones and twos?

Whole heap a people pon pavement –
whole heap a youts pon road.
How can a somebody know so much
people dem –
them all know each other?
Them nah noh each other –
all in them bastardise version
a them same uniform.
The same kinda different
got them lookin –
all the same
an'
tryin too hard – to look hard.

Eatin out on street
for the worl' to see
like them never nyam before –
like them noh raise –
like them noh raised at all –
like them nevah have no Mooma an'
no Poopa
to manners their manners.

Half a them nah dress right neither –
too cold –
mi see it.
Too hot –
mi see it.
Not enough clothes on –
not long enough clothes on –
gyal dem got more mout' than the boys...
heh
kinda remind me of –
me.

Cross the road
and look the white man butchers

where mi a go get mi meat from.
Lamb.

Fe him at home.

1.27.

SISTER   If I was a man –
nah – but *wait* –
if I was *my* man
truss it –
thass *right* –
I woulda been phonin *me* quick time
from time   '
for the longest time… right.

Even tho my mobile been on lock down
that don't matter –
that can't distract –
nu'un to stop him
flexin a text –
voicemailin me a little 'sorry' –
tryin a ting
try a ting –
try anything.
Just…
try man.

2.10.

DAD   'Smoddy phone.'

MUM   Thass my welcome back.

DAD   'Smoddy phone.'

MUM   My welcome home.

'Who?'

DAD   'Mi nah noh.'

(*Beat*.)

MUM	'Y'pick up?'
DAD	'Sleepin.'
MUM	'Butchu hear it.'
DAD	'Hmmph.'
MUM	'Butchu nah pick it up?'
DAD	'Woulda one a your people dem –'
MUM	'How yu know?'
DAD	'Mi noh.'

MUM   So him psychic now.
                       We inna psychic someting –
                       evidently –
                       but mi never noh –
                       nevah realise me husband secret talent.
                       Over all these long years.
                       H'evidently.
                       My husban' one a dem man who...
                       don't say much –
                       unless him haf to –
                       who don't say nuthin –
                       unless him want to...
                       Who nah pick up the phone –
                       cah him *psychic* to raas –

                       'We got lamb chops.'

DAD   'We got company.'

MUM   'Huh?'

DAD   'We got a smoddy at the door.'

MUM   I –
                       turn.
                       Mi
                       look.
                       He, right –
                       the shadow of some somebodies –

standin there –
for me to open.

I
see them –
them
see me –
them nod a uniformed, trained politeness
I look back – see me husband
strainin to see…

Him never psychic this one.

(*Beat*.)

[Iss the] Police.

SISTER   'Come home.'
What I thought was from my man
is from my mum.
'Come home. Now.'
One message from her.
And one *stink* message from Junior
from morning.
He think he's funny – carry on
thinks he's comedian – carry on
as my finger runs to find delete.
Now *thass* funny bruv.

'Come home. Now.'

(*Beat*.)

Deepak looks over –
knows not to ask –
he still in his own misery anyhow.
John concentrating on his eat out –
Jane only one to say –
'Where you goin?'
'… Home.'
Sally ears prick –

flicks her bottle-blonde shit –
gets the strength to speak in her disgrace –
'You sick?'
'… I'm sick.' (Of you.)
Sally on the –
'Aaah. You alright?'
Deepak attack now with the –
'How can she be alright – when she says
she's sick?'
Sally siddown sharp
pullin on her hair a mess.
John heads up with a –
'We'll let them know –
anything you want covered?'
Fe them to frigg up my work.
Hell no.
Log off – password padlock – quick-time.
'Hope you feel better'
then he's back to his burger –
they back to their work –
the air of the office politics
back to what it was.
I…
Leave.
2.13.

MUM   Bout –
can they come in?

They still there
lookin at me
lookin at them
they lookin past me at him
bout…
'Can they come in?'
Two a them Police cars
park outside
our yard.

Right outside
our yard.
… And all a my
whys?
All a my
who's
all a my
where's
all a my
what's
and whens and whyfors
rampaging all thru my –
mind
only come out as a quiet

… No.

Look back to my husband
who looks forward – at them.
We united on this one.

'Don't be bringin no Polices to my door.'
That was his first law.
'And if they come –
an' one a yous kids in trouble if they do –
don't let even a one a them in'
that was his second.
And the kids would eyes to the sky and
sigh
and
'no Dad'
and
'yes Dad'
and
bored a the lecture before it begin.
'Never trouble trouble till trouble trouble
yu.'
That was mine.
Maybe this someone else's trouble.
Bout.

'Can we come in.'
The law still outside
standin on our doorstep
waitin on a answer…

'No.'

(*Beat*.)

(*Beat*.)

Dark boots an' heavy shoes
inna my house.

On my carpet.

Dark boots
an' heavy shoes –
on my clean carpet
in my good room –
in my front room –
my visitor room –
my room fe best –
fe formal –
not even fe fambily.
Dark boots and heavy shoes –
beatin down my
for best carpet
without a second thought…
from them.
Outside shoes ent worn in this house –
an'
'no I don't wan' no cup a tea.'
An'
ennit for me to offer?
an'
'Yes, I am his wife –
his mother –
they my kids –
he my Son.'
And –

DAD

'Yes – I am ar husban'
their father –
an' no – mi nah want no cup a tea –
thass fe us to offer –
an' no
mi noh wan' fe sit. Neither.'

SISTER

If Mum took sick
Dad should be lookin after her.

Dad would ring.
Wouldn't stop ringin.

If Dad took sick
Mum would manage.
Always has.

Text her I'm comin –
phone Junior to see if he know more'n I do
but he doin what I do
thinkin he smart –
locked off his phone.

Leave him a stink message instead.

(MUM *is bewildered*.)

MUM

Him tink seh me sittin
is some kinda betrayal.
Can see it
how he look pon me – a flicker as me do it
behind he's eyes.
I catch it
an' dash it
cah mi ha'fe siddown
before mi drop down.

'… Mi dawta… Mi dawta.
Mek mi phone mi dawta.

I want to phone mi [*dawta*] – I have to
phone our – tell them we wan' phone our
[dawta] – I want her here – I want her
here.'

(*Beat*.)

'… How yu know iss him?'

(*Beat*.)

'How yu know – ?'

Them a chat bout
'eyewitness'
an'
'description'
an'
'ID' him a carry –
an'
seems that –
they gotta view
of my Son
of
who my Son is –
where my Son is
of
who them tink seh my Son is
and doin what.
… 1.30 – they say. Lunch break.
About – 1.30 – on the high street.
Near by the butchers.
A 'altercation'
a – 'attack' –
a – 'yout – another yout' –
they think.
Them a chat bout…
su'un su'un
them mout' move –
but me ear them juss…
rebel…

an'
refuse…
an'
try an' stop hear.

(*Beat*.)

I want mi dawta. Here.
Them –
offer them mobile
but
I look fe mi landline
can't dial –
husband do –
he can't say…
I do – only…
'Come home.
Come home now.'

2.07.
Say nu'un else.

Look to my husband
who stays standin.
All eyes on them
them who look more awkward than we do.
I –
shiver –
he –
offer them tea
they too keen in their trained acceptance
that breaks the silence
text book
how it should.

He stands
good an' straight
my man.

Like the good straight man him is
like the good straight man mi marry

asks them them sugar preference
then tells them... straight:

'I don't believe you.'

SISTER   Dad always said
                          'Don't bring no Polices back –
                          don't let no Polices in'
                          same thing he'd say bout white people –
                          Mum'd chip in with some
                          old-skool su'un bout –
                          'trouble an' trouble – reh teh teh'
                          but we never lissen good
                          we be bored by that bit –
                          truss mi.

                          So it odd.

                          Seein –
                          not a one
                          but a two piece a Police cars
                          outside our yard.
                          For all to see.
                          Obvious.
                          For all to know.
                          Blatant.
                          For all to chat bout.
                          Shame.

                          Mum gonna cuss.
                          Dad gonna be pissed.
                          They ent here for me –
                          so
                          it ent my arse
                          thass gonna get kicked –
                          Junior –
                          better have one piece a excuse.

MUM   I see that the too-sweet tea
                          don't sweet them.

See he sweet it too much.
On purpose.
How he do –
with people he don't like.
Them nah sey nu'un
bout his lack of belief.
Them nah sey nu'un
bout his nasty tea
too trained in a unnatural politeness
to let their guard...
slip.
They watch us.
We watch them.
As they sit sat
sip
swallow
and tink what part of they script
they gonna select next.

SISTER   ... Reh.
Shoes on in the front room.
They better be Police.
Boots on in the front room.

They better be brave dred.

Smell Dad's too-sweet tea a mile off
muss be poisonin them
with sugar.
Mum sat –
lookin shook.
Dad standin
lookin like he have to.
Su'un too quiet bout the house
su'un not right.
Step in – sock-foot
and see the two uniforms
and a plain clothes
sippin their too-sweet somethin.

MUM   'This our dawta.'

SISTER   Says Mum.
                       I don't bother to 'hi' a hello.
                       2.53.

MUM   I... uh...
                       Look to mi husban'
                       hold onto mi gurl.
                       She do what I do
                       if sense never leave me –
                       she look them up an' down –
                       sights them outside shoes inside
                       an' she ask an' she ask an' she h'ask an' –

SISTER   'How yu know iss him – how yu know he
                       was there – how yu know iss not some-
                       body who favour? How y'know he ent on
                       road – ent at he's girls – one a he's girls –
                       how yu don't know that? How y'know he
                       ent juss late? How y'know he ent with he's
                       spars –
                       Spars?
                       Friends – man dem – mates – bredrins –
                       no...
                       not a 'gang'.
                       Why you here?
                       Why you sittin here?
                       Why you in here sittin on *my* mum's good
                       sofa –
                       in *your* outside shoes –
                       drinking *my* dad's sweet tea –
                       an' askin bout my *brother* –
                       why you here? Why you – why you *here*?'

                       (*Beat.*)

                       (*Beat.*)

                       So they bring out their...
                       clear plastic bag

of a conversation stopper.
So all can –
clearly see
what they –
clearly
tryinta say.
Mum looks –
looks away.
Dad lookin at them
still.
I clock the bag
and its content
and –
deny.

'So it look like he's phone – what?
Nuff mans carry dem same piece a su'un.
So it look like he's phone – *what*?
My number last dial on it – so?
So it look like he's phone – *yeh* – that is
my number – yeh – that is his phone then.
So? And? *What?...*'

… What's with the brown on it?
Oh.
Blood.

… Since when does a mans bleed brown?

'… When the blood is old and dry.'

Oh.

(*Beat.*)

Why ent we…
where he is?

… Why ent we –
where he is –
why ent we gone?

Why ent we in one a your

flash pig cars
with your sirens on?
What if he's shook?

What if he's not sure –
and what the fuck you think he's family's
for?
What if he's callin –

for his Dad –
his Mum –
… Me?

(*Beat.*)

… And they sip their tea –
and they sat there sittin –
tryin to
pacify our worry
with a…

'There's no need to hurry,
there's no need to hurry.

There is no

need
to
hurry.'

… We already way too late.
… And never even know it.

PART TWO

SISTER   Dad went down to ID my brother.
I went down to support our dad.

Dad went in
I didn't have to follow.
But…

Brother had a –
birthmark.
Here.
Juss like me.
But his been
cut thru
with a chunk of him gone
now.
He had an eye
two.
Now he got juss one.
They try to pretty it up
mek it look like he winkin…
But
… you can't pretty up
whass horrific.
Y'not meant to.

His mout'
look like a clown –
now
wider than it should be.
It slashed so much on a one side
from there
to there.

That juss he's face.

Thass juss the ones that would mark him,
wouldn't kill him.

Apparently.

Thass juss the ones he'd haveta live with.
Have had to live with.

He have plenty little
like – uh – like –
(*gestures forearms*)
look like he a self-harmer
but proof he fought back.
Then they have to turn him
and
hold him
an'
lie him on his side
an'
so we could see – could see good
lookin hard to see.

Point of entry.
The killer cut.

You have to look hard
to look hard.

This was...
the smallest.
The cleanest.
The easiest to miss
part of it all.
Truss mi.
Juss –
round.
(*gestures*)
From the back –
those rules is broken then –
thru to –
(*gestures*)

punctured his...
su'un – important.
But.
Not no gash.
Not no not sure.
Not no random.
Juss a small
deep
sorta
round
sorta
hole.
In him.

Easy to miss.
Easy to miss.

Easy to miss.

(*Beat.*)

And our dad the kinda dad who...
Who...
don't say nuthin –
unless he –
who won't say anythin –
unless...
Dad tryin to say somethin.
Dad's tryin to say somethin
but
... nu'un won't [come out]...

I watch.
Watch him.
... He's embarrassed.
I watch his embarrassment.
I can't look away.

Where do it say –
this is part of it?
... Truss me.

They lift us back
in a unmarked ride,
tho I can still tell iss one of theirs.
And me an' Dad sit
in the back –
like kids
as they drive us home
havin to ask directions.
The only thing breakin the heavy silence.

And I still ent stopped
starin at Dad.
Dad still ent stopped
lookin away
and we pass the everyday
the life goes on
the
people goin about they business
the
people who don't know – won't know –
don't got no idea.

We pass the spot.
I ask –
to stop. Get let out and get out.
As they drive on.

Standin by the yellow an' blue murder
board
the battlefield where brother slain.
Alone.
Me on my own.
Cept for the boys in blue
guarding the pavement piece
I guess.
Watchin
the Police tape bouncing
in the breeze.
Too late.

Passerby passes by
don't look once
let alone twice
used to it.

Some too-old young men
in low-bats an' hoodies
holdin bunches of
proper flowers
not no garage shit
sight me
and say:
'… Sorry sis.
He was safe.'

Like I don't know.

Baby women
barely breakin their teens
upset
see me
upset
ask brazen as brazen baby women do
'Is it true he was your brother?'

(*Beat*.)

'Nah man – wrong'
she say
'if it was some skank little hoodrat then – '

That would be alright?

'He was nice'
she say
'[he] said I was ['nice'] – usedta clock him
inna mornins outside the Asian man
shop…
Coke an' crisp… '
She looks to the spot
starts singin some r'n'b tune
some dry r'n'b tune

as a gesture
dry lyrics
as a tribute.
Shit voice.
Shit song.
If she proper knew him
she woulda know
he was a bashment man.

A…
street shrine starts to stack up
flowers
candles
cards
T-shirts
tags
teddy bears
Coke an' crisp
the flag of our island
Garvey's colours of Africa –
a note from his form teacher
signed with a smile…
Shrine really start to pack up.

A baby mother puts down her contribution
steps back admires
nods me
knows me
her baby sleeps on
'Gonna mek it betta than
them mans dem
down them other ends'
she sey.
'This a proper shrine.
Bless.'
And she gone.
A sea –
of he's schoolpeeps
stand there.

Nuff.
In a heavy silence.
With their –
MP3 wires dangling
their
mobile phones
on silent
their schoolbags still slung
on their
uniformed backs.
The homegurls heng onto each other –
homeboys
hold each other up
as they silently shake
shook.
Hidin their faces
in each other's shoulders
witnessin somethin they shouldn't
and…
cry.

The press
pressin
the picturesque for a bite.
Their – blue-eyed reporters
shieldin their zeal
for a – 'good', 'urban' story
stepping into these sides
askin foolish questions
soundbitin so-called 'solutions'
in seconds.
Feelin brave askin a hard-lookin 'hoodie'
what he think.
Only to find
under the cloak of Adidas
is a brotha
whose eyes don't stop flowin.
Wet raw
with weepin.

But…
they don't show that bit tho.

Death usedta be for the old.

An' still the street shrine
propah packs up
stacks up
with Black on Black love.
Mum won't go.
Point-blank
won't go.

MUM   So they can look
and call me 'dignified'
look
and call me 'strong'
look
and see *me* cryin
look
glad it not them
look
and wonder where the smoke was
cos *su'un* muss have force the fire.
(*dry*) Right?
I don't got nuthin nice to say.
Nu'un polite
nu'un
broadcastable
nu'un
righteous
nu'un forgivin
juss pure…

SISTER   She don't say.
Mum won't go.
Point-blank.

She sittin as she was
as she has been
in her same spot in the front room

with some – Victim Support su'un su'un
sat by her now
who got it right.
With their shoes off.
But
makin no difference
to the difference we now got.
Can't make this difference
go away.

Dad – Dad's
takin the phone calls.
Bewildered by it.
Family doin family things
phonin
findin out
somebody gotta say
somebody gotta tellem.
Dad doin a –
bad
job of it
but...
Mum don't want no one round the house.
Not no one.

Sally, John, Deepak an' Jane
rock up on the doorstep.
Unannounced
unasked
uneasy.
Jane hidin behind John
Sally's eye wet,
Deepak bein brave
steps up an' says
'They've heard.
And they just wanted to say –
if there's anything
at any time
any a them
can do... '

Why Jane's playin shy I don't know
and who ask Sally fe bawl
she never know my brother
she don't even know me
and I look them
and I watch them
an' I see their unease
an' I say
'Iss alright.'
John not buyin it
says in a second
'Nah iss not.
We juss wanted you to know. Y'know?'
Which was… [nice].

They don't ask to come in.
They don't overstay.
Gimme a touch as they go –
John the only one to look back
seein me seein them leave.
And nods.
And leaves me watchin.

(*Beat.*)

(*Beat.*)

I lissen

and I hear…

(*Silence.*)

I hear – an juss get –

(*Silence.*)

Whole heap a witness
Polices say.

Whole heap a somebodies
on street.
Saw.
Whole heap a peeps
on road
was present.
But I lissen –
hard –
an' still I hear…

(*Silence*.)

Silence shoutin the loudest.
Cos it seem that
now no one wanna witness
what happened

to my Brother.

Mum wants to see his body.
Dad tell ar she don't.
Mum wants to see his body.
Dad tells her, 'Don't.'
Mum tells me

MUM   'I-wants-to-see-my-Son's-body.'

SISTER   I tell her –
               'She won't.'
               She looks on me and Dad
               like
               we the perpetrators now
               cuts her eye and asks

MUM   'You sure it was him?'

SISTER   'Yeh. It was.'

MUM   'How yu know?'

SISTER   Dad says, 'It was.'

MUM   'Y'see his mark?'

SISTER	I say… Yeh.
MUM	'Yu see his mark?'
SISTER	Dad says, 'Yeh' too.
MUM	'Y'sure it was him?'
SISTER	'Yeh. It was him, Mum.'
MUM	'Y'sure it was *him*?'
SISTER	Dad nods. Mum not missin a beat:
MUM	'Y'sure he was dead?'
SISTER	Support Officer says somethin quietly in Mum's ear. Mum stays eyes on me throwing out her bad looks.
MUM	'Y'sure he was *dead*?'
SISTER	Support Officer keeps sayin her su'un hard in Mum's ear gives Mum a touch keeps talking till Mum kisses her teeth at me looks away from me looks to the Support Officer and gives *her* a nod.

What did I do?

(*Beat.*)

Dad's done took
the phone off its hook
and left it there.
Hanging.
I'm told

not to touch it –
not to hook it back –
not to phone out –
not to answer it –
not to go near it –
Dad's had enough
'but – '
he don't wanna hear
'but – '
don't wanna hear me
'but – '
don't wanna hear what I got to say
… Dad's had enough.
But…

Su'un in the kitchen
startin to smell tho.
Mum don't care.
Dad don't wanna know.
But somethin in the kitchen
is startin to [stink] –
Dad don't want me in there –
'but – '
Dad don't want me – in there
'but – '
Dad – don't want me.

As he sits in the stink
comin from the bag
from the white man butchers
sittin on the side goin wrenk.

(*Beat.*)

My room ent holdin nuthin for me.
My room ent holdin [nuthin for me] –
it ent holdin nuthin for me now.
Left as I left it
this morning
when he was still asleep
in his room

this morning
when he was still –
in his room…
this morning.

So I go in he's.
He would kill me if he knew.

And it still stinks.

Of the sleep
of the sweat-off
of the young man
of… my brother.
I close back the door
to keep it in.
Sit on the floor –
finding a clean bit –

back to the wall and
wait…

It don't smell sweeter
like I tho't it would.
Still stinks as it did.
As bad as it did
and his bed's
as unmade as it was
and he's garms is
still spread all over
and he's computer's still on standby
cos he didn't give a fuck about goin green.
And he's burnt CDs is scattered
and he's pirate DVDs is lyin around
and he's books is unread
and he's mags ent as outta sight as he tho't
and he's weights
lie waitin
and he's too-strong-young-buck aftershave
lies open-top
and he's hair sheen…

stands alone
waitin on the shaved head
to come back.

And he's heroes look on
from their pinned point of view
as young and Black and dead as he is
now.

Fuck this cycle of shit.
And his poster of Halle
hangs over his bed
both of us clockin
it's as empty as it will be
now.
So I take a deep –
(*inhales*)
and don't wanna lose the strength
of his bedroom su'un.
Ever.

And the house is quiet…
y'know?
The house that never was…
is well quiet.

And I open his top drawer
boxers and socks
close it in case he know.
Open his second drawer –
tops an' tees
draw open his third…
sweat-tops sweatpants –
close it carefully.
… Juss in case he's watchin.

(*Beat.*)

Random don't happen to everybody.
So.
How come
'random' haveta happen to him?

This shit ent fair.

(*Beat*.)

Birds is silent
grievin as well.
Neighbourhood Stafs still
barkin the shit outta the area –
an' the sun –
the sun decided it's done for the day –
and this room…
(*inhales deeply*)

Close back his
drawer
close back his
door –
keep his stink in.
Step down the – too quiet stairs
past the stank Dad still sittin in
from the kitchen.
Pass the socked Support Officer
struggling –
in the best room
with our…

my

destroyed Mum.
And I…
step out.

Right.
Right.

End.

Other Titles in this Series